Batch R1231

R123113PG607713BVX00102B9781802695939 m
PERFECT   6.00X9.00 1)
Ordered by Ryan Williams For REPRINTS for C y
see email

R123113PG607713BVX00103B9781802750980 DASH DIET RECIPES: Healthy Eating fo
PERFECT   6.00X9.00   112   GLOSS   (1)
Ordered by Ryan Williams For REPRINTS for Chambersburg SSCC 79911 Ships Monday
see email

R123113PG607713BVX00104B9781802695953 The Best Mediterranean Cookbook : 50
PERFECT   6.00X9.00   112   GLOSS   (1)
Ordered by Ryan Williams For REPRINTS for Chambersburg SSCC 79911 Ships Monday
see email

R123113PG607713BVX00105B9781802920109 Friggitrice ad Aria: Nuove Ricette tutte It
PERFECT   6.00X9.00   112   GLOSS   (1)
Ordered by Ryan Williams For REPRINTS for Chambersburg SSCC 79911 Ships Monday
see email

R123113PG607713BVX00106B9781802750942 DASH DIET RECIPES: Eating Well for
PERFECT   6.00X9.00   112   GLOSS   (1)
Ordered by Ryan Williams For REPRINTS for Chambersburg SSCC 79911 Ships Monday
see email

R123113PG607713BVX00107B9781801979863 Hausgemachtes Pizza-Kochbuch
PERFECT   6.00X9.00   112   GLOSS   (1)
Ordered by Ryan Williams For REPRINTS for Chambersburg SSCC 79911 Ships Monday
see email

R123113PG607713BVX00108B9781802721065 Emotional Intelligence: How to Master So
PERFECT   6.00X9.00   114   GLOSS   (1)
Ordered by Ryan Williams For REPRINTS for Chambersburg SSCC 79911 Ships Monday
see email

R123113PG607713BVX00109B9781801979900 SANDWICH-REZEPTE
PERFECT   6.00X9.00   114   GLOSS   (1)
Ordered by Ryan Williams For REPRINTS for Chambersburg SSCC 79911 Ships Monday
see email

R123113PG607713BVX00110B9781802416404 BBQ Cookbook For Beginners: A Comple
PERFECT   6.00X9.00   114   GLOSS   (1)
Ordered by Ryan Williams For REPRINTS for Chambersburg SSCC 79911 Ships Monday
see email

R123113PG607713BVX00111B9781802148435 Spanish Vocabulary: Learn Spanish That I
PERFECT   6.00X9.00   116   GLOSS   (1)
Ordered by Ryan Williams For REPRINTS for Chambersburg SSCC 79911 Ships Monday
see email

R123113PG607713BVX00112B9781802413236 Amazing Dutch Oven Cookbook : Essent
PERFECT   6.00X9.00   116   GLOSS   (1)
Ordered by Ryan Williams For REPRINTS for Chambersburg SSCC 79911 Ships Monday
see email

Batch R12311300001B

R123113PG607713BVX00113B9781802533477 Intermittent Fasting for Women for begin
PERFECT   6.00X9.00   116   GLOSS   (1)
Ordered by Ryan Williams For REPRINTS for Chambersburg SSCC 79911 Ships Monday see email

R123113PG607713BVX00114B9781802838008 Renal Diet Cookbook for Absolute Begin
PERFECT   6.00X9.00   116   GLOSS   (1)
Ordered by Ryan Williams For REPRINTS for Chambersburg SSCC 79911 Ships Monday see email

R123113PG607713BVX00115B9781802416329 The Complete BBQ Cookbook : The Com
PERFECT   6.00X9.00   118   GLOSS   (1)
Ordered by Ryan Williams For REPRINTS for Chambersburg SSCC 79911 Ships Monday see email

R123113PG607713BVX00116B9781802890976 Vegan Recipes for Bodybuilding: Afford
PERFECT   6.00X9.00   118   GLOSS   (1)
Ordered by Ryan Williams For REPRINTS for Chambersburg SSCC 79911 Ships Monday see email

R123113PG607713BVX00117B9781802890952 Vegan Cookbook for Athletes 2021: Healt
PERFECT   6.00X9.00   118   GLOSS   (1)
Ordered by Ryan Williams For REPRINTS for Chambersburg SSCC 79911 Ships Monday see email

R123113PG607713BVX00118B9781667113494 COPYCAT RECIPES : Famous Collection
PERFECT   6.00X9.00   120   GLOSS   (1)
Ordered by Ryan Williams For REPRINTS for Chambersburg SSCC 79911 Ships Monday see email

R123113PG607713BVX00119B9781802930276 PASSIVE INCOME FOR BEGINNERS:
PERFECT   6.00X9.00   120   GLOSS   (1)
Ordered by Ryan Williams For REPRINTS for Chambersburg SSCC 79911 Ships Monday see email

R123113PG607713BVX00120B9781892501493 Bread machine recipes cookbook: The Gui
PERFECT   6.00X9.00   122   GLOSS   (1)
Ordered by Ryan Williams For REPRINTS for Chambersburg SSCC 79911 Ships Monday see email

R123113PG607713BVX00121B9781914395291 The Easy Meal-Prep Cookbook: Fast and
PERFECT   6.00X9.00   122   GLOSS   (1)
Ordered by Ryan Williams For REPRINTS for Chambersburg SSCC 79911 Ships Monday see email

R123113PG607713BVX00122B9781801839815 Intermittent Fasting and Autophagy: Disco
PERFECT   6.00X9.00   122   GLOSS   (1)
Ordered by Ryan Williams For REPRINTS for Chambersburg SSCC 79911 Ships Monday see email

R123113PG607713BVX00123B9781801979665 LIBRO DE RECETA DE HAMBURGUE
PERFECT   6.00X9.00   122   GLOSS   (1)
Ordered by Ryan Williams For REPRINTS for Chambersburg SSCC 79911 Ships Monday see email

Batch R12311300001B

R123113PG607713BVX00124B9781802882766 50 façons de faire du pain pour les début
PERFECT   6.00X9.00   124   GLOSS   (1)
Ordered by Ryan Williams For REPRINTS for Chambersburg SSCC 79911 Ships Monday
see email

R123113PG607713BVX00125B9781802946062 Bread Machine Recipes: A Complete Co
PERFECT   6.00X9.00   126   GLOSS   (1)
Ordered by Ryan Williams For REPRINTS for Chambersburg SSCC 79911 Ships Monday
see email

R123113PG607713BVX00126B9781802882926 Le livre de recettes pour la cuisson du poi
PERFECT   6.00X9.00   132   GLOSS   (1)
Ordered by Ryan Williams For REPRINTS for Chambersburg SSCC 79911 Ships Monday
see email

R123113PG607713BVX00127B9781802890914 Plant-Based Recipes for Athletes: Whole
PERFECT   6.00X9.00   132   GLOSS   (1)
Ordered by Ryan Williams For REPRINTS for Chambersburg SSCC 79911 Ships Monday
see email

R123113PG607713BVX00130B9781802946109 Bread Machine Recipes: A Bread Machin
PERFECT   6.00X9.00   138   GLOSS   (1)
Ordered by Ryan Williams For REPRINTS for Chambersburg SSCC 79911 Ships Monday
see email

R123113PG607713BVX00131B9781802946086 Bread Machine Recipes: A Complete Guid
PERFECT   6.00X9.00   140   GLOSS   (1)
Ordered by Ryan Williams For REPRINTS for Chambersburg SSCC 79911 Ships Monday
see email

R123113PG607713BVX00132B9781802946123 Keto Bread Cookbook: Easy, Quick And
PERFECT   6.00X9.00   146   GLOSS   (1)
Ordered by Ryan Williams For REPRINTS for Chambersburg SSCC 79911 Ships Monday
see email

R123113PG607713BVX00133B9781802932393 Las Aventuras de Pinocho Ilustrado
PERFECT   6.00X9.00   150   GLOSS   (1)
Ordered by Ryan Williams For REPRINTS for Chambersburg SSCC 79911 Ships Monday
see email

R123113PG607713BVX00134B9781802930191 FITNESS PROGRAM: How to Become
PERFECT   6.00X9.00   224   GLOSS   (1)
Ordered by Ryan Williams For REPRINTS for Chambersburg SSCC 79911 Ships Monday
see email

R123113PG607713BVX00136B9781991000521 Finding the Safe
PERFECT   5.25X8.00   42   GLOSS   (1)
Ordered by Ryan Williams For REPRINTS for Chambersburg SSCC 79911 Ships Monday
see email

R123113PG607713BVX00137B9781991000651 Grom Comp Day
PERFECT   5.25X8.00   42   GLOSS   (1)
Ordered by Ryan Williams For REPRINTS for Chambersburg SSCC 79911 Ships Monday
see email

5-Ingredient Recipes

Super Quick and Simple Budget-Friendly Recipes for Delicious Meals

Leslie Joy

work can be in any fashion deemed liable for any hardship or damages that may befall them after undertaking information described herein.

Additionally, the information in the following pages is intended only for informational purposes and should thus be thought of as universal. As befitting its nature, it is presented without assurance regarding its prolonged validity or interim quality. Trademarks that are mentioned are done without written consent and can in no way be considered an endorsement from the trademark holder.

TABLE OF CONTENTS

Introduction

Make healthy and easy meals fast using just five ingredients.

If you don't have a lot of time to cook, this book is for you.

Creating delicious and easy meals with only 5 ingredients is the new trend.

These 5 ingredients (or less) recipes are very fast and easy but taste like you put loads of time and effort into them. Each one needs just a handful of ingredients, plus salt, pepper, and cooking oil in some cases, so they won't be a strain on your family budget.

This book is all about the ingenious combination of a few ingredients. Their combination can produce amazing results and give you an explosion of flavor with a minimum of effort.

Many sweet and savory recipes with few ingredients are just waiting to be tried. Super easy, you'll make them quickly and everyone will be amazed.

Fancy a sweet treat but few ingredients at home?

Desserts with 3 ingredients, but also main courses that you will cook in no time while making it easy on your budget. Sometimes you just need to make the most of a few raw materials to prepare outstanding meals.

Recipes with only 5 ingredients are waiting for you, enjoy!

5-Ingredient Recipes

Cauliflower Toast with Avocado

Time required:
40 minutes

Servings: 03

INGREDIENTS

3 large eggs

3 big head cauliflower, grated

3 medium avocados, pitted and chopped

1 cup mozzarella cheese, shredded

Salt and black pepper, to taste

STEPS FOR COOKING

1. Preheat the oven to 420°F, then line a baking sheet with parchment.

2. Place the cauliflower in a microwave-safe bowl and microwave for about 7 minutes on high.

3. Spread on paper towels to drain after the cauliflower has completely cooled and press with a clean towel to remove excess moisture.

4. Put the cauliflower back in the bowl and stir in the mozzarella cheese and egg.

5. Season with salt and black pepper and stir until well combined.

6. Spoon the mixture onto the baking sheet in two rounded squares, as evenly as possible.

7. Bake for about 20 minutes until golden brown on the edges. 8. Mash

the avocado with a pinch of salt and
black pepper.

8. Spread the avocado onto the
cauliflower toast and serve.

Almond Butter Brownies

Time required:
30 minutes

Servings: 04

INGREDIENTS

1 scoop protein powder

2 tbsp. cocoa powder

1/2 cup almond butter, melted

1 cup bananas, overripe

STEPS FOR COOKING

1. Preheat the oven to 350 F/ 176 C, then spray the brownie tray with cooking spray.
2. Add all the ingredients into the blender, mix until smooth.
3. Pour batter into the prepared dish and bake in preheated oven for 20 minutes.
4. Serve and enjoy.

Pumpkin Pancakes

Time required:
20 minutes

Servings: 08

INGREDIENTS

2 squares puff pastry

6 tbsp pumpkin filling

2 small eggs, beaten

¼ tsp cinnamon

STEPS FOR COOKING

1. Preheat the Airfryer to 360 F and roll out a square of puff pastry.
2. Layer it with pumpkin pie filling, leaving about 1/4 -inch space around the edges.
3. Cut it up into equal-sized square pieces and cover the gaps with beaten egg.
4. Arrange the squares into a baking dish and cook for about 12 minutes.
5. Sprinkle some cinnamon and serve.

Kale Smoothie

Time required:
5 minutes

Servings: 02

INGREDIENTS

2 cups chopped kale
leaves

1 banana, peeled

1 cup frozen
strawberries

1 cup unsweetened
almond milk

4 Medjool dates,
pitted and chopped

STEPS FOR COOKING

1. Put all the ingredients in a food
    processor, then blitz until glossy and
    smooth.
2. Serve immediately.

Tiramisu Chia Pudding

Time required:
20 minutes

Servings: 01

INGREDIENTS

¼ cup Chia Seeds

2 tsp Instant Coffee

2 tbsp Coconut
Cream

¾ cup Water

1 tbsp Erythritol

1 tsp Powdered
Cinnamon

STEPS FOR COOKING

1. Combine all ingredients in a mason jar, then shake until well blended.
2. Chill for at least 20 minutes.

Apple - Lemon Bowl

Time required:
20 minutes

Servings: 02

INGREDIENTS

6 apples

3 tablespoons
walnuts

7 dates Lemon juice

1/2 teaspoon
cinnamon

STEPS FOR COOKING

1. Root the apples, then break them into
   wide bits.

2. In a food cup, put seeds, part of the
   lime juice, almonds, spices, and three-
   quarters of the apples. Thinly slice
   until finely ground.

3. Apply the remaining apples and lemon
   juice and make slices.

Bacon Mini Frittata

Time required:
40 minutes

Servings: 12

INGREDIENTS

1 cup chopped asparagus (about 7-8)

4 slices of bacon cut into cubes

2 tablespoons of chopped onions

8 eggs, beaten

1/2 cup (120 ml) coconut milk

Salt and pepper to taste

STEPS FOR COOKING

1. Preheat the oven to 350 degrees Fahrenheit (175 degrees Celsius).
2. Cook chopped bacon in a frying pan.
3. Mix all the chopped vegetables, cooked bacon, scrambled eggs, and coconut milk together in a large bowl.
4. Pour the mixture into muffin cups (makes 12 small quiches).
5. Bake for 25-30 minutes.

Chocolate Peanut Butter Shake

Time required:
5 minutes

Servings: 02

INGREDIENTS

2 bananas

3 Tablespoons peanut butter

1 cup almond milk

3 Tablespoons cacao powder

STEPS FOR COOKING

1. Combine all the ingredients in a blender until smooth, then serve.

Ham Muffins

Time required:
25 minutes

Servings: 04

INGREDIENTS

3 oz ham, chopped

4 eggs, beaten

2 tablespoon
coconut flour

½ teaspoon dried
oregano

¼ teaspoon dried
cilantro

Cooking spray

STEPS FOR COOKING

1. Spray the muffin's molds with cooking spray.

2. In a bowl, mix the beaten eggs, coconut flour, dried oregano, cilantro, and ham.

3. When the liquid is homogenous, pour in it the prepared muffin molds.

4. Bake the muffins for 15 minutes at 360F

5. Chill the cooked meal well and only after this remove it from the molds.

Nori Salmon Handroll

Time required:
10 minutes

Servings: 01

INGREDIENTS

*2 ounces wild
canned salmon*

1 toasted nori sheet

1/4 avocado

1 cucumber

1 green onion

STEPS FOR COOKING

1. Slice avocado and cucumber and finely chop the green onion.
2. Put the nori paper on a cutting board, and layer the avocado, fish, 2 slices of cucumber, and green onion.
3. Wrap the paper around.

Breakfast Cheesy Sausage

Time required:
25 minutes

Servings: 01

INGREDIENTS

1 pork sausage link, cut open and casing discarded

½ teaspoon thyme

½ teaspoon sage

½ cup mozzarella cheese, shredded

Sea salt and black pepper, to taste

STEPS FOR COOKING

1. Mix the sausage meat with thyme, sage, mozzarella cheese, sea salt, and black pepper.

2. Shape the mixture into 2 equal-sized patties and transfer to a hot pan.

3. Cook for about 5 minutes per side and dish out to serve.

Crusty Grilled Corn

Time required:
25 minutes

Servings: 04

INGREDIENTS

2 corn cobs

1/3 cup Vegenaise

1 small handful of Cilantro

½ cup breadcrumbs

1 teaspoon lemon juice

STEPS FOR COOKING

1. Preheat the gas grill on high heat.
2. Add corn grill to the grill and continue grilling until it turns golden-brown on all sides.

Creamy Potato Spread

Time required:
25 minutes

_____

Servings: 06

INGREDIENTS

1 lb sweet potatoes, peeled and chopped

¾ tbsp fresh chives, chopped

½ tsp paprika

1 tbsp garlic, minced

1 cup tomato puree

Pepper and Salt

STEPS FOR COOKING

1. Add all ingredients except chives into the inner pot and stir well.

2. Seal pot with the lid and cook on high for 15 minutes.

3. Once done, allow to release pressure naturally for 10 minutes, then release remaining using quick release. Remove lid.

4. Transfer instant pot sweet potato mixture into the food processor and process until smooth.

5. Garnish with chives and serve.

Garlic and Kale Platter

Time required:
15 minutes

Servings: 04

INGREDIENTS

1 bunch kale

2 tablespoons olive oil

4 garlic cloves, minced

STEPS FOR COOKING

1. Carefully tear the kale into bite-sized portions, making sure to remove the stem.

2. Discard the stems.

3. Take a large-sized pot and place it over medium heat.

4. Add olive oil and let the oil heat up, then add garlic and stir for 2 minutes.

5. Add kale and cook for 5-10 minutes.

6. Serve!

Almond Bread

Time required:
40 minutes

Servings: 20

INGREDIENTS

6 eggs, separated

1/4 teaspoon cream of tartar

3 teaspoons baking powder

4 tablespoons butter, melted

1 1/2 cups almond flour

1/4 teaspoon salt

STEPS FOR COOKING

1. Preheat the oven to 375 F. Grease 8*4-inch loaf pan with butter and set aside. Add egg whites and cream of tartar in a large bowl and beat until soft peaks form.

2. Add almond flour, baking powder, egg yolks, butter, and salt in a food processor and process until combined.

3. Add 1/3 of egg white mixture into the almond flour mixture and process until combined. Now add the remaining egg white mixture and process gently to combine.

4. Pour batter into the prepared loaf pan, then bake for 30 minutes. Slice and serve.

Mozzarella Chips

Time required:
10 minutes

___

Servings: 08

INGREDIENTS

*4 phyllo dough
sheets*

*4 oz mozzarella,
shredded*

*1 tablespoon olive
oil*

STEPS FOR COOKING

1. Place 2 phyllo sheets in the pan and
    brush it with a sprinkle of mozzarella.
2. Then cover the cheese with 2
    remaining phyllo sheets.
3. Brush the top of Phyllo with olive oil
    and cut on 8 squares.
4. Bake the chips for l0 minutes at 363F
    or until they are light brown.

Broccoli Stir Fry

Time required:
25 minutes

Servings: 02

INGREDIENTS

1 tablespoon coconut oil

2 cups broccoli florets

1 tablespoon low-sodium soy sauce

¼ teaspoon garlic powder

Ground black pepper, as required

STEPS FOR COOKING

1. In a large pan, melt the coconut oil over medium heat and stir in the broccoli.

2. Cover the pan, then cook for 10 minutes, stirring occasionally.

3. Stir in the soy sauce and spices and cook for about 5 minutes.

4. Serve hot.

Wrapped Plums

Time required:
5 minutes

Servings: 08

INGREDIENTS

*2 ounces prosciutto,
cut into 16 pieces*

4 plums, quartered

*1 tablespoon chives,
chopped*

*A pinch of red
pepper flakes,
crushed*

STEPS FOR COOKING

1. Wrap each plum quarter in a
   prosciutto slice, arrange them all on a
   platter, sprinkle the chives and pepper
   flakes all over.

2. Serve.

Fried Apple

Time required:
20 minutes

Servings: 04

INGREDIENTS

1 cup of coconut oil
¼ cup date paste
2 tablespoons ground cinnamon
4 apples, peeled and sliced, cored

STEPS FOR COOKING

1. Place a large-sized skillet over medium heat.
2. Add oil and allow it to heat. Add date paste and cinnamon and stir.
3. Add the apples and fry until crispy, for 5-8 minutes.
4. Serve and enjoy!

Paprika Sweet Potato

Time required:
21 minutes

Servings: 02

INGREDIENTS

2 sweet potatoes

2 teaspoons sweet paprika

1/2 teaspoon oregano, dried

1 teaspoon chili powder

1 teaspoon chives, chopped

1/2 cup of water

STEPS FOR COOKING

1. Pour water into the instant pot and insert a steamer rack.
2. Put potatoes on the rack and close the lid.
3. Set Manual mode (High pressure) and cook for 11 minutes. Then use quick pressure release.
4. Transfer the potatoes to the plate, cut into halves, sprinkle the rest of the ingredients on top, and serve.

Tomato Basil Spaghetti

Time required:
25 minutes

Servings: 04

INGREDIENTS

15-ounce cooked
great northern
beans

10.5-ounces cherry
tomatoes halved

1 small white onion,
peeled, diced

1 tablespoon minced
garlic

8 basil leaves,
chopped

2 tablespoons olive
oil

1-pound spaghetti

STEPS FOR COOKING

1. Take a large pot half full with salty
   water, place it over medium-high
   heat, bring it to a boil, add spaghetti
   and cook for 10 to 12 minutes until
   tender.

2. Then drain spaghetti into a colander
   and reserve 1 cup of pasta liquid.

3. Take a large skillet pan, place it over
   medium-high heat, add oil, and when
   hot, add onion, tomatoes, basil, and
   garlic and cook for 5 minutes until
   vegetables have turned tender.

4. Add cooked spaghetti and beans, pour
   in pasta water, stir until just mixed
   and cook for 2 minutes until hot.

5. Serve straight away.

Worcestershire Pork Chops

Time required:
15 minutes

Servings: 03

INGREDIENTS

2 tablespoons
Worcestershire
sauce

8 oz pork loin chops

1 tablespoon lemon
juice

1 teaspoon olive oil

STEPS FOR COOKING

1. Mix up together Worcestershire sauce, lemon juice, and olive oil.

2. Brush the pork loin chops with the sauce mixture from each side.

3. Preheat the grill to 395F.

4. Place the pork chops in the grill and cook them for 5 minutes.

5. Then flip the pork chops on another side and brush with the remaining sauce mixture.

6. Grill the meat for 7-8 minutes more.

Baked Chicken Wings

Time required:
60 minutes

Servings: 04

INGREDIENTS

2 lbs chicken wings

1 tbsp. lemon-pepper seasoning

2 tbsp butter, melted

4 tbsp olive oil

STEPS FOR COOKING

1. Preheat the oven to 400 F.
2. Toss chicken wings with olive oil.
3. Arrange chicken wings on a baking tray and bake for 50 minutes.
4. In a small bowl, mix together lemon pepper seasoning and butter.
5. Remove wings from oven and brush with butter and seasoning mixture.
6. Serve and enjoy.

Broccoli Bacon Salad with Onions and Coconut Cream

Time required:
40 minutes

Servings: 06

INGREDIENTS

1 pound of broccoli

4 small red onions or 2 large slices

20 bacon, cut into small pieces

1 cup coconut cream

Salt, to taste

STEPS FOR COOKING

1. Cook the bacon first, then cook the onions in the bacon fat.
2. Cook the broccoli florets.
3. Add bacon chunks, onions, and cauliflower florets, along with coconut cream and salt to taste.
4. Serve at room temperature.

Thyme and Lemon Couscous

Time required:
15 minutes

Servings: 06

INGREDIENTS

.25 cup Chopped parsley

1.5 cup Couscous

2 tbsp. Chopped thyme

Juice and zest of a lemon

2.75 cup Vegetable stock

STEPS FOR COOKING

1. Take out a pot and add in the thyme, lemon juice, and vegetable stock. Stir in the couscous after it has gotten to a boil and then take off the heat.

2. Allow sitting covered until it can take in all of the liquid. Then fluff up with a form.

3. Stir in the parsley and lemon zest, then serve warm.

Sage Salmon Fillet

Time required:
25 minutes

_____

Servings: 01

INGREDIENTS

4 oz salmon fillet

½ teaspoon salt

1 teaspoon sesame oil

½ teaspoon same

STEPS FOR COOKING

1. Rub the fillet with salt and sage.
2. Place the fish in the tray and sprinkle it with sesame oil.
3. Cook the fish for 25 minutes at 365F.
4. Flip the fish carefully onto another side after 12 minutes of cooking.

Eggs Baked in an Avocado

Time required:
17minutes

Servings: 02

INGREDIENTS

1 avocado

2 egg yolks

*2 teaspoons olive oil
or coconut oil*

*Salt, pepper, spices /
other herbs to taste*

STEPS FOR COOKING

1. Preheat the oven to 400 ° F.
2. Cut the avocado in half. You don't need the core.
3. Break the eggs into a bowl.
4. Scoop out each egg yolk and place half an avocado.
5. Pour 1 teaspoon of olive oil over each avocado egg yolk.
6. Bake for 12 minutes.
7. Sprinkle with salt and pepper and whatever herbs and spices you want to add.

Shrimp Ginger Cucumber with Fried Rice

Time required:
15 minutes

Servings: 01

INGREDIENTS

1 large cucumber, peeled and sliced into round slices

10-15 shrimp / large shrimp

1 teaspoon grated fresh ginger

Salt and pepper to taste

Coconut oil for cooking

STEPS FOR COOKING

1. Put a tablespoon of coconut oil in a frying pan over medium heat.
2. Add ginger and cucumber and sauté for 2-3 minutes.
3. Add shrimp and cook until pink.
4. Add salt to taste and serve.

5 Ingredients Pasta

Time required:
40 minutes

Servings: 05

INGREDIENTS

1 (25 oz.) jar marinara sauce

Olive oil, as needed

1 pound dry vegan pasta

1 pound assorted vegetables, like red onion, zucchini, and tomatoes

¼ cup prepared hummus

Salt, to taste

STEPS FOR COOKING

1. Preheat the oven to 400 degrees F, then grease a large baking sheet.

2. Arrange the vegetables in a single layer on the baking sheet and sprinkle with olive oil and salt.

3. Transfer into the oven and roast the vegetables for about 15 minutes.

4. Boil salted water in a large pot and cook the pasta according to the package directions.

5. Drain the water when the pasta is tender and put the pasta in a colander.

6. Mix together the marinara sauce and hummus in a large pot to make a creamy sauce.

7. Stir in the cooked vegetables and pasta to the sauce and toss to coat well.

8. Dish out in a bowl and serve warm.

French Onion Soup

Time required:
40 minutes

Servings: 06

INGREDIENTS

5 tablespoons butter

500g brown onion medium

4 drops liquid stevia

4 tablespoons olive oil

3 cups beef stock

STEPS FOR COOKING

1. Put the butter and olive oil in a large pot over medium-low heat and add onions and salt.

2. Cook for about 5 minutes and stir in stevia.

3. Cook for another 5 minutes and add beef stock.

4. Reduce the heat to low, then simmer for about 25 minutes.

5. Dish out into soup bowls and serve hot.

Cream of Mushroom Soup

Time required:
36 minutes

_____

Servings: 02

INGREDIENTS

2 cups cauliflower florets

1 2/3 cup plain almond milk

1 tsp onion powder

1/2 tsp EVOO

1 1/2 cups button mushrooms, diced

1/2 yellow onion, chopped

STEPS FOR COOKING

1. Boil the cauliflower in a pot with almond milk and onion powder. Season with salt and pepper, then drop to a simmer and cook until the cauliflower is just tender 5-7 minutes. Blend this mixture until very smooth in a blender.

2. Sauté the mushrooms and onions in a separate pan in the oil. Cook on high heat, so that the vegetables can gain color and the mushrooms will leach out some of their liquid.

3. Add the cauliflower puree to the mushrooms after 7-8 minutes, then bring to a boil. Lower the heat and cover, then cook until the soup is thick and creamy, 10-12 minutes.

4. Season and serve.

Grilled Eggplant Steaks

Time required:
25 minutes

Servings: 02

INGREDIENTS

4 Roma tomatoes, diced

8 ounces cashew cream

2 eggplants

1 tablespoon olive oil

1 cup parsley, chopped

1 cucumber, diced

Salt and pepper to taste

STEPS FOR COOKING

1. Slice eggplants into three thick steaks, drizzle with oil, and season with salt and pepper.
2. Grill in a pan for 4 minutes per side.
3. Top with remaining ingredients.
4. Serve and enjoy!

Coconut Chicken

Time required:
5 minutes

Servings: 04

INGREDIENTS

6 oz chicken fillet
¼ cup of sparkling water
1 egg
3 tablespoons coconut flakes
1 tablespoon coconut oil
1 teaspoon Greek Seasoning

STEPS FOR COOKING

1. Cut the chicken fillet into small pieces (nuggets).
2. Then crack the egg in the bowl and whisk it.
3. Mix up together egg and sparkling water.
4. Add Greek seasoning and stir gently.
5. Dip the chicken nuggets in the egg mixture and then coat in the coconut flakes.
6. Melt the coconut oil in the skillet and heat it up until it is shimmering.
7. Then add prepared chicken nuggets.
8. Roast them for 1 minute from each or until they are light brown.

INGREDIENTS	STEPS FOR COOKING
	9. Dry the cooked chicken nuggets with the help of the paper towel and transfer them to the serving plates.

Shrimp and Broccoli

Time required:
17 minutes

Servings: 02

INGREDIENTS

1/2 lb shrimp

1 tsp fresh lemon
juice

2 tbsp butter

2 garlic cloves,
minced

1 cup broccoli florets

Salt

STEPS FOR COOKING

1. Melt butter in a pan over medium heat, then add garlic and broccoli to the pan and cook for 3-4 minutes.

2. Add shrimp and cook for 3-4 minutes.

3. Add lemon juice and salt, then stir well.

4. Serve and enjoy.

Tofu Nuggets with Barbecue Glaze

Time required:
35 minutes

Servings: 09

INGREDIENTS

32 ounces tofu

1 cup quick vegan barbecue sauce

STEPS FOR COOKING

1. Set the oven to 425F.
2. Next, slice the tofu and blot the tofu with clean towels, then slice and dice the tofu and completely eliminate the water from the tofu material.
3. Stir the tofu with the vegan barbecue sauce, and place the tofu on a baking sheet.
4. Bake the tofu for fifteen minutes. Afterward, stir the tofu and bake the tofu for an additional ten minutes.
5. Enjoy!

Yummy Turkey Meatballs

Time required:
25 minutes

Servings: 04

INGREDIENTS

¼ yellow onion, finely diced

1 14-oz can of artichoke hearts, diced

1 lb. ground turkey

1 tsp dried parsley

1 tsp oil

4 tbsp fresh basil, finely chopped

Pepper, and salt to taste

STEPS FOR COOKING

1. Grease a cookie sheet, then preheat the oven to 350F.

2. On medium fire, place a nonstick medium saucepan and sauté artichoke hearts and diced onions for 5 minutes or until onions are soft.

3. Remove from fire and let cool.

4. Meanwhile, in a big bowl, mix with hands parsley, basil, and ground turkey. Season to taste.

5. Once the onion mixture has cooled, add it into the bowl and mix thoroughly.

6. With an ice cream scooper, scoop ground turkey and form it into balls, make around 6 balls.

7. Place on prepped cookie sheet, pop in the oven and bake until cooked through around 15-20 minutes.

8. Remove from pan, serve and enjoy.

Healthy Poached Trout

Time required:
10 minutes

Servings: 02

INGREDIENTS

*1 8-OZ boneless,
skin-on trout fillet*

*2 cups chicken broth
or water*

2 leeks, halved

6-8 slices lemon

*Salt and pepper to
taste*

STEPS FOR COOKING

1. On medium fire, place a large nonstick skillet and arrange leeks and lemons on a pan in a layer. Cover with soup stock or water and bring to a simmer.

2. Meanwhile, season trout with pepper and salt, then place trout on a simmering pan of water. Cover and cook until trout is flaky, around 8 minutes.

3. In a seeing platter, spoon leek and lemons on the bottom of the plate, top with trout, and spoon sauce into the plate. Serve and enjoy.

Avocado Cucumber Soup

Time required:
20 minutes

Servings: 03

INGREDIENTS

1 large cucumber,
peeled and sliced

¾ cup water

¼ cup lemon juice

2 garlic cloves

6 green onion

2 avocados, pitted

Salt and pepper

STEPS FOR COOKING

1. Add all ingredients into the blender and blend until smooth and creamy.
2. Place in refrigerator for 30 minutes.
3. Stir well and serve chilled.

Oregano and Pesto Lamb

Time required:
25 minutes

Servings: 04

INGREDIENTS

2 pounds pork shoulder, boneless and cubed

¼ cup olive oil

2 teaspoons oregano, dried

¼ cup lemon juice

3 garlic cloves, minced

2 teaspoons basil pesto

Salt and black pepper to the taste

STEPS FOR COOKING

1. Heat up a pan with the oil over medium-high heat, then add the pork, and brown for 5 minutes.

2. Add the rest of the ingredients, cook for 20 minutes more, tossing the mix from time to time, divide between plates and serve.

Buttery Shrimp

Time required:
20 minutes

Servings: 04

INGREDIENTS

1 1/2 lbs shrimp

1 tbsp Italian seasoning

1 lemon, sliced

1 stick butter, melted

STEPS FOR COOKING

1. Add all ingredients into the large mixing bowl and toss well. 2. Transfer the shrimp mixture to a baking tray.

2. Bake at 350 F for 15 minutes.

3. Serve and enjoy.

Salted Caramel Chocolate Cups

Time required:
7 minutes

Servings: 12

INGREDIENTS

¼ teaspoon sea salt
granules

1 cup dark chocolate
chips, unsweetened

2 teaspoons coconut
oil

6 tablespoons
caramel sauce

STEPS FOR COOKING

1. Take a heatproof bowl, add chocolate chips and oil, stir until mixed, then microwave for 1 minute until melted, stir chocolate and continue heating in the microwave for 30 seconds.

2. Take twelve mini muffin tins, line them with muffin liners, spoon a little bit of chocolate mixture into the tins, spread the chocolate in the bottom and along the sides, and freeze for 10 minutes until set.

3. Then fill each cup with ½ tablespoon of caramel sauce, cover with remaining chocolate and freeze for another 2salt0 minutes until set.

4. When ready to eat, peel off liner from the cup, sprinkle with sauce, and serve.

Warm Peach Compote

Time required:
5 minutes

Servings: 04

INGREDIENTS

*4 peaches, peeled
and chopped*

1 tbsp water

½ tbsp cornstarch

1 tsp vanilla

STEPS FOR COOKING

1. Add water, vanilla, and peaches into the instant pot.

2. Seal pot with lid and cook on high for 1 minute.

3. Once done, allow to release pressure naturally. Remove lid.

4. In a small bowl, whisk together 1 tbsp of water and cornstarch and pour into the pot and stir well.

5. Serve and enjoy.

Vanilla Custard

Time required:
20 minutes

Servings: 02

INGREDIENTS

8 egg yolks

1 cup unsweetened almond milk

1 teaspoon vanilla extract

10 stevia extract drops (optional)

6 tablespoons melted coconut oil or unsalted butter

STEPS FOR COOKING

1. In a large, heatproof bowl, whisk the eggs, and then add the milk, vanilla, and honey.
2. Slowly mix in the melted coconut oil.
3. Now place this bowl over a pan of simmering water.
4. Insert a cooking thermometer into the pudding. Once the thermometer reads 140°F, remove the custard from the water bath.
5. Serve it warm or chilled.

Peanut Brittle

Time required:
25 minutes

Servings: 04

INGREDIENTS

*1 cup peanuts,
salted and roasted*

2 oz butter

*3 oz swerve
sweetener*

1 tsp vanilla extract

STEPS FOR COOKING

1. Line a cookie sheet with wax paper and spread out the peanuts.

2. Using a small saucepan over medium heat, combine the butter, sweetener, and vanilla.

3. Cook until it reaches the caramelized stage and is deep brown in color. Do not undercook to avoid making your brittle grainy.

4. Pour the caramel over the spread peanuts and let it cool for 30 minutes to an hour. Once it hardens, break into pieces before serving.

Watermelon Mint Popsicles

Time required:
25 minutes

Servings: 08

INGREDIENTS

20 mint leaves, diced

6 cups watermelon chunks

3 tablespoons lime juice

STEPS FOR COOKING

1. Add watermelon in a food processor along with lime juice and then pulse for 15 seconds until smooth.

2. Pass the watermelon mixture through a strainer placed over a bowl, remove the seeds and then stir mint into the collected watermelon mixture.

3. Take eight Popsicle molds, pour in prepared watermelon mixture, and freeze for 2 hours until slightly firm.

4. Then insert popsicle sticks and continue freezing for 6 hours until solid.

5. Serve straight away.

Creamy Strawberries

Time required:
5 minutes

Servings: 04

INGREDIENTS

6 tablespoons almond butter

1 tablespoon Erythritol

1 cup milk

1 teaspoon vanilla extract

1 cup strawberries, sliced

STEPS FOR COOKING

1. Pour milk into the saucepan.
2. Add Erythritol, vanilla extract, and almond butter.
3. With the help of the hand mixer, mix up the liquid until smooth and bring it to a boil.
4. Now, remove the mixture from the heat and let it cool.
5. The cooled mixture will be thick.
6. Put the strawberries in the serving glasses and top with the thick almond butter dip.

Coconut Bars

Time required:
45 minutes

Servings: 02

INGREDIENTS

1 large scoop protein powder, vanilla flavored

4 oz. dark chocolate chips, unsweetened

1 cup coconut, flaked

¾ cup coconut oil, melted

1½ cups macadamia nuts, raw

STEPS FOR COOKING

1. Using an 8-inch pan, cover with baking paper or a non-stick mat.

2. In a food blender set to high, blend the macadamia nuts and coconut oil until evenly mixed.

3. Combine the protein powder, chocolate chips, and coconut until mixed thoroughly.

4. Transfer the batter to the prepped pan and freeze for half an hour.

5. After it's set, slice into 14 individual bars. 6. Thaw for 10 minutes before serving.

Boston Baked Beans Candy

Time required:
60 minutes

Servings: 06

INGREDIENTS

2 cup peanuts, raw
1 cup allulose
½ cup water

STEPS FOR COOKING

1. Place the entire ingredients in a large skillet. Cook over moderate heat until the water is evaporated, stirring every now and then.

2. Pour the mixture on a large-sized cookie sheet and bake in the oven for 20 minutes at 325°F. Break apart, if required.

Chocolate Rice

Time required:
20 minutes

Servings: 04

INGREDIENTS

1 cup of rice
1 tbsp cocoa powder
2 tbsp maple syrup
2 cups almond milk

STEPS FOR COOKING

1. Add all ingredients into the inner pot of the instant pot and stir well.
2. Seal pot with lid and cook on high for 20 minutes.
3. Once done, allow to release pressure naturally for 10 minutes, then release remaining using quick release. Remove lid.
4. Stir and serve.

Greek Yogurt Muesli Parfaits

Time required:
10 minutes

Servings: 04

INGREDIENTS

4 cups Greek yogurt

1 cup whole wheat muesli

2 cups fresh berries of your choice

STEPS FOR COOKING

1. Layer the four classes with Greek yogurt at the bottom, muesli on top, and berries.

2. Repeat the layers until the glass is filled, then place in the fridge for at least hours to chill.

CPSIA information can be obtained
at www.ICGtesting.com
Printed in the USA
BVHW011734040621
R12311300001B/R123113PG607638BVX00075B/1